essentials
bible study

a deeper look at foundational topics of the faith

essentials
bible study

greg laurie

NAVPRESS
Discipleship Inside Out®

KERYGMA
PUBLISHING

ALLEN
DAVID
BOOKS

NAVPRESS

Discipleship Inside Out®

NavPress is the publishing ministry of The Navigators, an international Christian organization and leader in personal spiritual development. NavPress is committed to helping people grow spiritually and enjoy lives of meaning and hope through personal and group resources that are biblically rooted, culturally relevant, and highly practical.

For a free catalog go to www.NavPress.com or call 1.800.366.7788 in the United States or 1.800.839.4769 in Canada.

contents

Getting Started

WE LIVE TODAY in information overload. There's far more knowledge available than we can absorb, let alone use. How do we know what's essential? Well, we can start with the things that will save our lives and the ones that make the difference between lives that flourish and lives that wither.

When we get on an airplane, someone always reminds us how the oxygen masks work, even though on any given flight we probably won't need them. Someone does this because on those rare occasions when passengers need to know how to use the masks, they *really* need to know.

The basic truths about God are even more important than that because they make the difference between flourishing and withering every day. And although they may not prevent us from physical death indefinitely, they can save us from a fate worse than death. Even if we think we know these basic truths, it's a good idea to go over them on a regular basis and ask, *How is this relevant to my life today? How can this make the crucial difference? What do I need to do about this?*

What you think about God has everything to do with how you will live your life. Your view of God will determine how you will react to what comes your way in life. (*Essentials* 6)

This study guide offers you a chance to think over the essentials of the Christian faith on your own or with a group of friends. You'll talk about God the Father, Jesus Christ, the Holy Spirit, heaven, hell, angels and demons, how we grow more mature in our faith, and what's going to happen when world history comes to a dramatic end. Whether you're a new believer or you've been around for years, these essentials are relevant to what's going on in your life right now. And because our world bombards you with distorted words and images about God, heaven, angels, demons, and the rest, this is a good chance to refocus on what's real and what's Hollywood. This study is based on the book *Essentials: Foundational Topics for Christians in Today's World*, by Greg Laurie.

At the beginning of each study session, you'll see the chapters of *Essentials* that you should read before your group meets. However, this study is designed to work even if you don't have time to read the book. As long as you have a Bible, you'll be fine. (You will, however, get more out of it if you read *Essentials* as you go along.)

Using This Study On Your Own

Ideally, you'll read the relevant chapters of *Essentials* before you dig into the questions for each session. Don't feel you must hurry to put down answers for all of the questions. If God is talking to you through one question, stay there and pray about it or write all that comes to you. This isn't a task to complete; it's a chance for you and God to talk about your life. If you skip some questions but you've been with God, that's what matters.

Using This Study with a Group

Again, ideally, you'll read the relevant chapters of *Essentials* before each meeting. Even better, read the chapters and spend some time thinking about answers to the questions before you meet. Better still, write your answers before the group meets. Then when you meet, don't just share what you've written — discuss it. Questions and different views are okay. You can certainly have a productive discussion without prior preparation, but you'll get much more out of the study if you make time for at least the reading at home.

Do establish a discussion leader. This person's job is to keep the conversation moving and decide when to go to the next question. He or she doesn't need to have the answers. If you are chosen for this role, see the Leader's Notes at the end of this guide. There are tips for guiding a discussion as well as ideas for individual questions.

Sometimes you may find it helpful to have someone read aloud the text between the questions. That text includes excerpts from *Essentials* that help to frame the questions. Reading aloud is especially helpful if people haven't had time to read the material on their own and write answers to the questions.

Do read aloud the Bible passages, whether you are looking them up in your Bible or they are printed in this book.

Finally, be as honest as you can with the members of your group. If you want to grow spiritually, you will greatly benefit from having other people who know what's going on with you and are supporting you, praying for you, and challenging your thinking.

The Real God

> To prepare for this discussion,
> please read chapters 1 and 2 of *Essentials*.

MORE THAN TWO hundred years ago, the French philosopher Voltaire said, "God made man in His image, and man returned the favor." Humans have always preferred to design their own gods rather than worship the One who actually exists. We love to customize our iPods, iPads, iPhones, and iTunes to suit our tastes, and many of us prefer an iGod too — programmed, personalized, saying what we want Him to say, doing what we want Him to do. We edit out the tracks we don't like and keep the ones we do.

Here's the trouble with a custom-designed god: It isn't real. Some people think that "real" doesn't exist — that we create our own realities. They're wrong. We influence our realities, but there's some bedrock out there that exists whether we want it or not. God is the biggest mountain of that bedrock. We can ignore or reimagine Him all we want, but that's deluding ourselves. (If you want to try to create your own reality where gravity doesn't exist and you jump off a building to prove it, good luck.)

Some of what we know about God can be learned by closely observing the world around us, but much of it we know only

Notes and Observations

because God has chosen to reveal Himself. The record of God's self-revelation is the Bible. In this session, we'll investigate what the God of the Bible is truly like.

1. How is God portrayed or discussed in movies, television shows, and Internet videos that you have seen? Give some examples.

The Bible portrays God as:

- *Omniscient* (He knows everything.)
- *Omnipresent* (He is present everywhere, but He is not the same as the world He has created.)
- *Omnipotent* (He is all-powerful. He can do anything that doesn't contradict His nature. For example, He can't die, as that would contradict His eternal nature.)
- *Sovereign* (Nothing happens that He doesn't cause or at least allow for His own purposes.)
- *Truth* (He is the final standard of what is true and false.)
- *Holy* (He hates evil and separates Himself from it.)
- *Righteous and Just* (He is committed to what is right; He hates injustice.)
- *Good* (He is the final standard of goodness, and all He does is worthy of approval.)
- *Love* (He isn't just loving; He Himself is love.)

That's a long list, so let's think about what difference each of these truths about God means for your life. First, **God knows everything.**

God's knowledge is as infinite and eternal as He is. What God knows now He has always known and will always know. . . .

God knows and remembers everything about everyone who has ever lived or will live. There is never the slightest lapse in His memory. He never forgets anyone or anything. . . .

Psalm 147:4 (NIV) tells us something even more amazing. It says of God that "He determines the number of the stars *and calls them each by name*" (emphasis added). . . .

Not only does He know all of this information about stars and galaxies and nebulas, He knows about *you*. As I mentioned, Jesus said, "The very hairs on your head are all numbered" (Matthew 10:30). . . .

God knows about every little bird that falls to the ground. Why did Jesus bring those two points — about birds and the hairs on our head — to our attention?

Because He wanted to reassure us that the Father cares about every detail of our lives. He said, "So don't be afraid; you are worth more than many sparrows" (Matthew 10:31, NIV).

This awesome God who created the universe and numbers the stars is interested in you. What bothers you? What concerns you? What makes your heart ache? What brings tears to your eyes? It is of concern to God. (*Essentials* 19–21)

2. a. Read Psalm 139:1-4. What are some things God knows about you?

b. What difference does it make to you that God knows all this?

Next, **God is present everywhere.**

3. Read Psalm 139:7-12. What difference does it make to you that God is everywhere—with you, with the people you're concerned about, anyplace you might run to?

God is all-powerful and sovereign. Nothing happens that He doesn't cause or at least allow for His own purposes.

> Your needs or requirements are never a drain on God's resources. You would never—in a trillion lifetimes—need more than God can supply. The Bible says that God is "able to do immeasurably more than all we ask or imagine, according to his power that is at work within us" (Ephesians 3:20, NIV).
>
> So consider your circumstances right now. Maybe you're overwhelmed by tragedy, grief, sorrow, confusion, uncertainty, or worry. Then again, maybe you are bound by an addiction of some kind. It could be an addiction that has grown so powerful it has turned into a lifestyle, and you feel as though you will never be free from it. I want you to know that the all-knowing, all-powerful, ever-present God is here to help you. (*Essentials* 26)

4. When have you experienced the help of the all-knowing, all-powerful, ever-present God? If you can't think of a time, do you need His help? Do you believe He's there to give it?

Horrible tragedies can tempt us to question whether God is *both* all-powerful *and* completely good, loving, and just. Consider these passages:

I know that the Lord is great,
And our Lord is above all gods.
Whatever the Lord pleases He does,
In heaven and in earth. (Psalm 135:5-6)

Remember my affliction and roaming,
The wormwood and the gall.
My soul still remembers
And sinks within me.
This I recall to my mind,
Therefore I have hope.

Through the Lord's mercies we are not consumed,
Because His compassions fail not.
They are new every morning;
Great is Your faithfulness.
"The Lord is my portion," says my soul,
"Therefore I hope in Him!"

The Lord is good to those who wait for Him,
To the soul who seeks Him.
It is good that one should hope and wait quietly
For the salvation of the Lord. . . .

Let him give his cheek to the one who strikes him,
And be full of reproach.
For the Lord will not cast off forever.
Though He causes grief,
Yet He will show compassion
According to the multitude of His mercies.
For He does not afflict willingly,
Nor grieve the children of men.

To crush under one's feet
All the prisoners of the earth,
To turn aside the justice due a man
Before the face of the Most High,

Or subvert a man in his cause —
The Lord does not approve.

Who is he who speaks and it comes to pass,
When the Lord has not commanded it?
Is it not from the mouth of the Most High
That woe and well-being proceed? (Lamentations 3:19-26,30-38)

In the second of these passages (from a book appropriately called Lamentations), the writer is grieving over the destruction of Jerusalem, the burning of God's own temple, and the deaths of thousands of his friends and neighbors, God's chosen people. He's coming to grips with the fact that the all-powerful God allowed this.

5. a. Where in the passages do you see the writers saying, "God is all-powerful and in control of what happens"?

b. Where in the Lamentations passage do you see the writer saying, "God is completely good, loving, and committed to justice"?

c. What does the writer of Lamentations think we should do when terrible things happen?

d. How do you respond to what he says?

The same God who declares Himself to be good promises in Romans 8:28 that He causes all things to work together for good for those that love Him and are the called according to His purpose.

We hear that verse invoked a lot. But have we ever thought it all the way through? A better translation of that verse says, "All things are working together for good to those who love God and are the called according to His purpose." In other words, it's in process. All things are working together, right now, for eventual good. (*Essentials* 34–35)

6. What's the difference between saying, "The death of this child is good," and, "God is working, even in the death of this child, for the eventual good of those who love Him"?

Next, **God is holy.** The Bible says His holiness (His utter purity and hatred of evil) should motivate us to "a wholesome dread of displeasing Him. '*Oh Lord, You are so good. You are so holy. I want to live in such a way that I bring honor to Your name*'" (*Essentials* 33).

7.   a. What do you think about "a wholesome dread" of dis- pleasing God? Can you have a wholesome dread of God and also trust Him with your deepest concerns? Explain.

b. How might a wholesome dread of God affect the way we live?

Lastly, **God is love.**

[God] is *not* the Hollywood version of love. What do these people in Hollywood know about love? "So-and-so is now with so-and-so. They are the beautiful couple. They are the powerful couple." Oh, and by the way, they probably won't be together for more than a few months before they drift off for other beautiful, powerful people.

God's love isn't fickle.

God's love isn't dependent on how attractive we are.

God's love doesn't hinge on our performance.

God says, "Yes, I have loved you with an everlasting love; therefore with lovingkindness I have drawn you" (Jeremiah 31:3).

What's more, God doesn't just talk about love. He has demonstrated it to us, as the Scripture says: "But God demonstrates His own love toward us, in that while we were still sinners, Christ died for us" (Romans 5:8).

God is love, and God is holy. Perhaps in these two qualities we can see all the attributes of God. In His holiness He is unapproachable. In His love He approaches us. (*Essentials* 36)

8. How do you want this discussion of God's attributes to affect the way you deal with life this week?

9. Take time to thank God for each of His attributes. Think of reasons you are genuinely grateful for each of them. If you find that an attribute is hard to be grateful for, tell God honestly why that's the case. You can use the following incomplete sentences to

guide your prayer on your own, or if you're meeting with a group, you can take turns each completing a sentence. (But give people the freedom to say something else to God about their given attribute.)

- Lord, thank You that You know everything because

  _____.

- Lord, thank You that You are present everywhere because

  _____.

- Lord, thank You that You have unlimited power because

  _____.

- Lord, thank You that You are in control because

  _____.

- Lord, thank You that You are the standard of what is true

  because _____.

- Lord, thank You that You are holy because

  _____.

- Lord, thank You that You are righteous and just because

  _____.

- Lord, thank You that You are good because

  _____.

- Lord, thank You that You are love because

  _____.

Jesus: God in the Flesh

2

To prepare for this discussion,
please read chapter 3 of *Essentials*.

THE ROCK OPERA *Jesus Christ Superstar* depicts Jesus as a gifted human overwhelmed by the demands of all the beggars and sick people who want His healing touch. He tells the mob to heal themselves because He can't fix everyone's problems. The political situation in Jerusalem is too much for Him to handle, and He's hurt by the apostles' failure to understand Him.

Everybody seems to have an opinion about Jesus. Some think He was a wise teacher of ethics or spirituality. Some say He was a revolutionary, championing the cause of the poor against the Romans and rich Jews. Some sentimentalize Him. Some dismiss Him.

Who is He really? That's what we'll explore in this session.

1. Think of movies and artwork you've seen that depict Jesus. How do they depict Him? What impression of Him do you get from them?

Notes and Observations

If you want to know what God is like, take a long look at Jesus Christ, because Jesus is God in human form. If you want to see all of the wonderful attributes of God embodied and put on display, look at Jesus. When Jesus walked this earth, He wasn't a mere representative of God; He was God Himself walking among us. . . . He wasn't a glorified man, but God in human form, "God with skin on."

He embodied all the attributes of God that we've already talked about . . . yet He was also a man who walked our planet, breathed our air, and felt our pain.

He was so wise that He could predict the future events of the world.

He was so humble that He could get on His knees and wash His friends' dirty feet.

He was so powerful that He could calm the wind and waves with a word.

And He was so approachable that children climbed into His arms.

As someone has said, Jesus was God spelling Himself out in language we could all understand. (*Essentials* 44)

2. Read the following passages. What statements in each passage convey that Jesus is fully God?

John 1:1-5

Luke 5:17-26

Colossians 1:15-20

3. a. What does Colossians 1:20-22 say Jesus accomplished when He died on the cross?

    b. What does it mean to say that Jesus made peace through His shed blood? Peace between whom and whom?

At a point in history, Jesus became fully human. When He lived on earth, He walked until He was tired, He got physically hungry and thirsty, He felt anger and sorrow, He bled real blood, He experienced real human agony, and finally He died as a man in that His body ceased to function. He didn't just *appear* to be a man; He *was* a man.

During His time on earth, He didn't cease to be fully God, but He did lay aside the privileges and many of the powers of God. The all-powerful God became a helpless infant. The all-knowing God went through a learning process as He grew up (see Luke 2:52). The God who is present everywhere limited Himself to a body that could be in only one place at a time. He "emptied Himself, taking the form of a bond-servant, and being made in the likeness of men" (Philippians 2:7, NASB).

4. Read Hebrews 4:15-16. How does Jesus' experience as a human affect the way He views and treats us?

5. What are some of the weaknesses you experience that you're glad Jesus understands?

6. How does the writer of Hebrews want us to respond to the fact that Jesus understands what human life is like?

Jesus referred to God in heaven as "Father":

Jesus answered them, "My Father has been working until now, and I have been working." Therefore the Jews sought all the more to kill Him, because He not only broke the Sabbath, but also said that God was His Father, making Himself equal with God. (John 5:17-18)

Jesus has been the Son of God eternally; when we put our faith in Him, we are adopted as the Father's children and as Jesus' brothers and sisters.

7. How was it different for Jesus to call God "Father" than it is for us to call Him "Father"? Why does this matter?

If He wasn't God, then His death on the cross wasn't of any great significance.

There were many men who died on Roman crosses 2,000 years ago, and one of them happened to be named Jesus. But there was only one Man who died on a cross *who was God in human form, atoning for the sin of the world, and then bodily raised again from the dead.* (*Essentials* 49)

He was despised and rejected —
> *a man of sorrows, acquainted with deepest grief.*
We turned our backs on him and looked the other way.
> *He was despised, and we did not care.*

Yet it was our weaknesses he carried;
> *it was our sorrows that weighed him down.*
And we thought his troubles were a punishment from God,
> *a punishment for his own sins!*
But he was pierced for our rebellion,
> *crushed for our sins.*
He was beaten so we could be whole.
> *He was whipped so we could be healed.*
All of us, like sheep, have strayed away.
> *We have left God's paths to follow our own.*
Yet the LORD laid on him
> *the sins of us all.* (Isaiah 53:3-6, NLT)

8. How does this passage from Isaiah describe what Jesus went through for you? What words and phrases stand out to you?

9. Isaiah says, "We have left God's paths to follow our own." Give some examples of paths that even pretty good people follow that aren't God's paths.

Why was the suffering Isaiah describes necessary? Why did God have to become human and die for us instead of just staying in heaven and saying we're forgiven? Because every sin has consequences. God is holy and perfectly just, so it would violate His nature to just shrug and say evil acts don't matter, rebellion against the rightful King doesn't matter. It matters. So God satisfied His justice by paying the consequences Himself, on the cross.

10. What does it say about God that He was willing to go through what Isaiah describes for your sake?

11. *Jesus Christ Superstar* portrays Jesus as overwhelmed, frustrated, and hurt. Do you think Jesus ever felt overwhelmed, frustrated, and hurt? Do you think that's an adequate depiction of Jesus? Explain.

Jesus Christ is not only with us, but . . . He actually comes and makes His home in the human heart that welcomes Him. Jesus said in John 14:23, "If anyone loves Me, he will keep My word; and My Father will love him, and We will come to him and make Our home with him."

God wants to make His home with you. He doesn't want to just stop by as a house guest or pay you a visit or have a nice little chat. He wants to move in. He wants to indwell you and transform you from the inside out.

He wants you to know that no matter what happens on these sometimes-dark roads that we walk on this side of heaven, we are never alone. (*Essentials* 57)

12. How do you feel about being transformed from the inside out? Is that something you want? Something that seems unnecessary? Something that makes you uncomfortable?

13. If you're studying on your own, write out a prayer to Jesus, telling Him what your life is like right now and thanking Him for being with you in the midst of it. If you're with a group, share an area of your life where you need to know that God is with you or tell about a part of you that you're asking Him to transform. As a group, pray for each other about those things.

The Holy Spirit and You 3

To prepare for this discussion,
please read chapters 4 and 5 of *Essentials*.

IN THE ORIGINAL *Star Wars* film from 1977 (now called *Episode IV: A New Hope*), Obi-Wan Kenobi tries to teach Luke Skywalker to move objects blindfolded and without touching them by tapping into "the Force." Obi-Wan says, "The Force is what gives a Jedi his power. It's an energy field created by all living things. It surrounds us and penetrates us. It binds the galaxy together."

When the Bible speaks of the Holy Spirit, many people imagine something like the Force: impersonal, generated by the universe or by God, something we can tap into and control if we learn and practice the right techniques. But this is not remotely what the biblical writers have in mind. In this session, we'll examine who the Holy Spirit really is.

1. Why do you think the Force is such an appealing idea to so many people?

Notes and Observations

We've seen that Jesus is God, and the Father is God, but Jesus isn't the same as the Father. The Holy Spirit is also God, but He isn't just another manifestation of the Father or the Son. When early Christians studied what the Bible teaches about the Father, the Son, and the Holy Spirit, they came up with the term *Trinity* to describe what the Bible teaches.

Doesn't it say in Deuteronomy 6:4 that "the LORD our God, the LORD is one"? Yes. And so He is. The Lord our God is one God. We worship and serve one God, not multiple gods. We aren't polytheistic; we are monotheistic. And yet the Bible clearly teaches that God is a Trinity.

We're not talking here about modes or manifestations of the same Persons, but rather three Persons who are all simultaneously active. In other words, the Father is not the same Person as the Son. And the Son is not the same Person as the Holy Spirit. There is one God, and this true God exists in three distinct, co-equal, co-eternal Persons. Not three Gods, but one. One substance, in perfect harmony. (*Essentials* 60)

2.   a. Read Matthew 3:13-17. Where do you see God the Son active in this scene? What does He do?

b. Where do you see God the Father active in this scene? What does He do?

c. Where do you see God the Holy Spirit active in this scene? What does He do?

d. How can we see in this scene that the Holy Spirit isn't just Jesus or the Father in another guise?

So how is the Holy Spirit different from the Force? First of all, Jesus consistently refers to the Spirit as "He," not "it" (see John 14:15-17; 16:8). The Holy Spirit is a Person with intelligence, emotion, and will. For example, He loves and can be grieved (see Ephesians 4:30).

3. How does it affect the way we deal with the Holy Spirit if we think of Him as a Person rather than an impersonal force?

Luke compares the Spirit to a mighty rushing wind and to fire. These are word pictures to convey the idea of power whose effects are visible even though the powerful Person is not. (In the same way, Jesus calls Himself "the door" [John 10:7,9] and Psalm 91 says God will give us refuge under His wings, but Jesus isn't a literal door and the Father isn't a bird.)

Jesus calls the Spirit the "Helper" (John 14:16), also translated as "Counselor" or "Advocate." The word means "one called alongside to help, counsel, defend." The Holy Spirit comes to live inside everyone whose faith is in Christ (see verse 17).

4. Have you ever experienced the Holy Spirit's helping or counseling you? If so, give an example.

In John 16:7-10, Jesus says the Holy Spirit is the one who convicts or convinces people that they are sinners in need of God's forgiveness and God's righteousness because the alternative is judgment.

> The Holy Spirit takes the message of the death and resurrection of Jesus, shows us it is true, and convinces us that we need to turn to God. Without the convicting power of the Spirit, you would never have come to Jesus. The Spirit shows you that you need God, that you need the salvation of Jesus Christ. There is nothing that I or any preacher, teacher, or author in the world could say to convince you of those things. It takes the power of the Spirit Himself.
>
> When I find myself praying for a nonbeliever, then, I will say, "Lord, convict this person by your Holy Spirit." I can certainly tell someone Jesus has made my life richer and better, and that I have great joy and peace in knowing God and having my sins forgiven. And that individual might think, *Well that's fine for you.* But what that person needs to realize is that he or she is a sinner, in desperate need of a Savior.
>
> I can't convince them of that.
>
> But guess what?
>
> The Holy Spirit is able to do that. That is His work, and His specialty. (*Essentials* 64)

5. If the Holy Spirit is the one who convinces people that they are sinners in need of salvation, what do you think our role is in drawing people to Christ? (For instance, how should we pray? Is it our fault if we tell someone about Jesus and they don't come

to faith? Is it okay if we just don't tell people and rely on the Spirit to convict them?)

The Holy Spirit is also the one who empowers us to develop Christlike love. In Galatians 5:22-23, Paul says "the fruit of the Spirit" is love that is defined by such characteristics as joy, peace, patience, goodness, kindness, faithfulness, and self-control.

> The way you can determine whether or not I am a follower of Jesus won't be because I simply say so. You will know I belong to Jesus because of the evidence you see in my life. And that evidence is sometimes called spiritual fruit.
>
> Fruit, of course, doesn't grow overnight; it takes time. (*Essentials* 83)

If people are filled with the Holy Spirit's power, we can see it evidenced primarily by the way they are forgiving to those who wrong them, sexually pure until they're married, faithful and kind to their spouse, patient and firm with their children, and so on.

6. How is this evidence of the Spirit's power different from the power of the Force in *Star Wars*? How does it compare to other ways you've heard people talk about the Spirit's power?

The Holy Spirit needs our cooperation in order to produce fruit in and through us. The way we cooperate with the Holy Spirit is to "abide" in Jesus (see John 15:1-8), which means to live all day, every day in conversation and communion with

Him — "to stay close to Him. To consciously depend on Him in a thousand situations throughout your day. Fruit will come as a result of this relationship with the Lord who loves you" (*Essentials* 85).

7. What are some practical ways you go about staying close to Jesus and depending on Him during your day? (Or if you have trouble doing this, what are the barriers you face and the questions you have?)

8. a. Read Romans 8:26-27. How does the Holy Spirit help us pray?

    b. Is this helpful for you to know? If so, how is it helpful?

9. Read John 14:26. The Holy Spirit also helps us understand the Bible and remember what it says. How do you think that should affect the way we study the Bible?

10. a. We haven't covered anywhere near all of the important things the Holy Spirit does for us. We haven't touched on spiritual gifts, for example. But as you look back over the

things we have covered, which one or two of the Holy Spirit's activities are you most grateful for?

b. Which one would you most like to understand better or experience more of in your current situation?

c. What steps can you take to cooperate with the Holy Spirit in that area?

11. The Holy Spirit is eager to fill you. All you have to do is ask—and cooperate. If you're meeting with a group, ask the Holy Spirit to fill each person. Ask Him to help and counsel you, to develop love in you, to pray in you for things you don't even know you need.

There are lots of good songs that praise the Holy Spirit and invite Him to come and fill you. Consider singing or playing one or more of them.

The Truth About Heaven

4

To prepare for this discussion,
please read chapters 6 through 8 of *Essentials*.

THE LATE SCIENCE-FICTION writer Isaac Asimov once wrote,

> I don't believe in an afterlife, so I don't have to spend my whole life fearing hell, or fearing heaven even more. For whatever the tortures of hell, I think the boredom of heaven would be even worse.[1]

Is he right? Is heaven boring? Not at all! What is it really like, and what difference does it make to our lives here on earth? That's what we'll explore in this session.

1. What images and notions about heaven can we find in popular media?

The Bible presents heaven as:

- An actual place, not a metaphor, ideal, or state of mind
- God's dwelling
- A city and a garden
- Even more real than this world, which is full of copies and shadows of what is in heaven

2. Read Revelation 21:10–22:5. What can we learn from this passage about what heaven is like? List everything you observe.

3. What do you think the precious stones and gold convey about heaven?

Revelation depicts heaven as a city. In the first century AD, people thought cities were the best places to be. (The wilderness was just plain dangerous.)

> Think of a perfect city where there is no crime, where everyone loves everyone, where the very streets and walls and sidewalks and buildings are translucent and glow with an inner radiance.
>
> Cities have culture. Cities have art, music, goods, services, events, and restaurants. Restaurants in heaven? Why not? We know there will be feasting there. . . .
>
> I think about Jerusalem at sunset, bathed in a golden light. Or Paris in springtime. (*Essentials* 107)

Also, Jesus refers to heaven as "Paradise" (Luke 23:43). In the first century, that word referred to a king's garden.

If you were a relatively impoverished person and were unexpectedly given the privilege of stepping inside the walled and well-tended garden of a king, you would be overwhelmed by that experience. The fragrance and beauty of it all would blow your circuit breakers.

So "paradise" was a reference point for people — the best human language could do. (*Essentials* 104)

4. How do you respond to the idea of a city of gold and jewels, filled with light and good people and a royal garden — and especially God Himself? What parts of Revelation's picture of heaven are you most drawn to? Would you prefer more space from other people or something wilder than a garden?

C. S. Lewis said,

All the things that have ever deeply possessed your soul have been hints of heaven — tantalizing glimpses, promises never quite fulfilled, echoes that died away just as they caught your ear. If I find in myself a desire which no experience in this world can satisfy, the most probable explanation is I was made for another world. Earthly pleasures were never meant to satisfy, but to arouse, to suggest, the real thing.[2]

5. What are some of the desires you've had that this world couldn't satisfy? (If you can't think of any such desires, do you think you're missing something, or is that just normal for some people?)

God is going to give you a brand-new body, but it won't be unrelated to your existing body. The blueprint for your eternal, glorified body is in the body you now possess. It's already there. . . .

For all its similarities, however, there will be wonderful differences.

When we get to the other side, our minds and our memories will be clearer than they have ever been before. . . .

No more physical disabilities. No signs of age. No sinful tendencies. (*Essentials* 115–116)

6. Read 1 Corinthians 15:43-44. Why is it important that we will have bodies and not be disembodied souls? What's good about having a body?

7. What changes do you look forward to in a glorified body?

Contrary to what Asimov said, we won't be bored in heaven. We'll enjoy being in God's glorious presence and worshipping Him (see Revelation 15:2-4), yet heaven will also be a place of productivity:

We wonder if we will be able to perhaps finish some of the tasks that remain uncompleted on earth. Maybe you had dreams that were shattered here that will in some sense be fulfilled there. Who is to say that God would not allow us to complete what He inspired us to start on the other side?

Remember that verse in Philippians? "He who began a good work in you will carry it on to completion until the day of Christ Jesus" (Philippians 1:6, NIV). God is all about finishing what He begins. (*Essentials* 120)

8. What are some of the unfulfilled dreams and uncompleted works that you hope to pursue for God's glory in heaven?

9. Many biblical passages depict heaven as a feast shared with those faithful who have gone before us (see Isaiah 25:6-8; Revelation 19:6). Why is feasting a good picture of heaven?

10. Who do you look forward to spending time with in heaven, feasting together or doing good work together?

11. There are good earthly reasons to think about heaven like this on a regular basis. Read Colossians 3:1-10. What reasons for setting our minds on things above, in heaven, does Paul give in this passage?

12. Paul lists many harmful habits that setting our sights on heaven should help us break free of. Describe how our destiny in heaven is inconsistent with . . .

Idolatry (making something other than God the primary interest, goal, love, or fear that drives us)

Coveting or greed (always wanting more, never being content with our possessions, status, spouse, or whatever)

Anger, meanness, and gossip

13. How can you cultivate the kind of focus on heaven that leads to a better life on earth? What helps you do that consistently?

14. Take some time to thank God for what awaits you in heaven. Thank Him for the specific things about heaven that mean the most to you. Praise Him for the glories of heaven. If you like, read aloud one or more of the heavenly worship songs from Revelation (4:8; 5:9-14; 15:3-4) or use one of them as a guide for your own words of worship.

Angels, Demons, and Hell

5

To prepare for this discussion,
please read chapters 9 through 11 of *Essentials*.

PEOPLE FEEL FREE to joke about hell. Comedian Woody Allen said, "Hell is the future abode of all people who personally annoy me." But there is a hell—a real hell—and it's no joke.

Angels and demons are real too, and they're not quite like the ways they're portrayed in popular media. In this session, we'll explore what the Bible really says about angels, demons, and hell.

1. How are hell and demons portrayed in movies and on television? (Think of some portrayals that are meant to make viewers laugh and some that are meant to frighten.)

2. Read Luke 16:19-31. How does Jesus describe the rich man's experience in Hades? Note the key words and phrases.

3. Why has the rich man been sentenced to this destiny?

4. The passage says there's a gulf between the place of torment and the place of comfort after death, and people are stuck with the destiny they've chosen in their earthly lives. Do you think people have enough information in this life to choose wisely about their eternal destiny? Explain. (Consider verses 28-29.)

Some people will say, "That's just not right. How could a God of love create a place called hell?"

The truth is, it is *because* He is a God of love that He created a place called hell. There are terrible injustices in this life and wrongs done that people should never get away with. And though they may escape the long arm of the law, they will never escape the long arm of God.

Justice will be done, and that justice will be final and complete.

Beyond all of that, however, hell was not made for people. Jesus said hell was created for the devil and his angels. It was never God's intention to send a person to hell, and He does everything He can to keep people out of hell.

But in the final analysis, it's our choice.

God has given to you and me a free will. I have the ability to choose, and God will not violate that. If you want to go to heaven, my friend, you will, if you put your faith in Christ. If you want to go to hell, you will. That is really your choice.

J. I. Packer wrote,

> Scripture sees hell as self-chosen. Hell appears as God's gesture of respect for human choice. All receive what they actually choose. Either to be with God forever worshipping Him or without God forever worshipping themselves. . . .[3]

In the end, we get what we most truly want. (*Essentials* 153–154)

5. How does hell's existence affect the way you view God? For instance, does it make Him seem harsh? Does it seem wrong to you that average people (not just those who commit unusually horrific crimes) go to hell? Explain.

The devil (Satan) and his demons are fallen angels. Before we look at the fallen ones, let's consider what an angel is.

While angels aren't human and have never been human, they sometimes take on human form, appearing as young men. By the way, there is no instance in the Bible of an angel appearing as a woman. It's funny, because our culture loves to use that word *angel* in a feminine sense. We'll say, "Oh, she is as pretty as an angel," or, "She sings like an angel." And often in religious art through the years, angels have been portrayed as female. In the Bible, however, when they take on a human form, it's always male. . . .

They're an elite fighting force, like the Navy SEALs. When the SEALs are dispatched on a mission, they go in, take care of business, and you rarely hear about it. It's not publicized. You don't know the names of the SEALs that did thus and so. You may read about the success of a given mission, but you never learn any of the details.

Like the SEALs, angels are sent out on missions all the time. They are "ministering spirits" who protect, deliver, guide, and bring messages from God. You don't need to engage them, and you don't need to try to communicate with them. Just step back and let them do their jobs, the work that God has called them to do. (*Essentials* 161–162)

6. What do you learn about angels from the following passages?

Isaiah 6:1-3

Luke 1:5-20

Luke 24:1-8

Acts 10:1-8

Acts 12:6-11

Hebrews 1:14

\

Revelation 19:9-10

There are military-like ranks among angels. God sometimes calls in the archangel Michael when lower-ranking angels need help. For instance, once when the prophet Daniel was praying, a fallen angel hindered one of God's angels from responding. After quite a delay, the angel finally showed up and said,

> Do not fear, Daniel, for from the first day that you set your heart to understand, and to humble yourself before your God, your words were heard; and I have come because of your words. But the prince of the kingdom of Persia withstood me twenty-one days; and behold, Michael, one of the chief princes, came to help me. (Daniel 10:12-13)

7. How should knowing about the warfare between God's angels and the devil's angels affect the way we pray? How should it affect the way we respond when answers to our prayers are delayed?

Believers aren't always protected from death and injury, are we? What about the times when the lion's mouth isn't closed? What about when someone doesn't narrowly miss that brush with death? What about when death takes us unexpectedly? Does that mean the angels missed their opportunity or were asleep on the job?

No, it means they have another mission now.

Angels did not determine the time when I was born, nor will they determine the time when I'm going to die. That is up to God. Up until the time of our passing, the role of the angel is to guide, to protect, or possibly redirect us. But when the time has come for us to enter into eternity, the role of the angel is to give us an escort into the presence of God [see Luke 16:22]. (*Essentials* 172)

8. How do you think we should relate to angels, if at all? Should we try to seek them out? Talk to them? Why?

The risk of trying to contact angels is that you might end up with the wrong kind. Fallen angels — or demons — can masquerade as the good guys. Their objectives are to hinder God's purposes and do Satan's work — to steal, kill, and destroy (see John 10:10).

Some people wonder how a God of love could create someone as horrible as the devil.

But God did not create the devil as we know him today.

The Lord created a spirit being, a mighty angel known as Lucifer, or "son of the morning." Lucifer, however, exercised the free will God had given him and rebelled against his creator. In so doing, he chose to be God's adversary and became Satan. The devil, then, was not created by God. The devil became what he is by his own volition.

On the other hand, God certainly allowed it. (*Essentials* 177)

9.   a. Read Ezekiel 28:12-19. How does this passage describe Lucifer before his fall?

b. According to Ezekiel, what flaws in Lucifer's character led him to rebel against God?

c. What does Isaiah 14:15-16 add to our understanding of how Lucifer (the morning star) became Satan (the adversary)?

Having led a third of God's angels into rebellion with him, Satan set out to bring down the human species, too. He tempted Eve to disbelieve God's promise and disobey His command (see Genesis 3:1-7).

If she ate of this fruit, she would become a goddess and know as much as heaven knew. In fact, wasn't it just a little bit strange that God was holding out on her, keeping something back from her? If God really loved her, He would let her have this marvelous fruit, wouldn't He?

Satan will say the same thing to us: "If God really loved you, He would let you do whatever you want to do. If God really loved you, He would allow you to chase after whatever passion interests you. If God really loved you, He wouldn't have allowed this to happen to you." That is what he was doing with Eve. He was challenging the Word of God, and he was challenging God's love for her. (*Essentials* 186)

10. a. What are some ways Satan has said to you, "If God really loved you, then He _____"?

b. What helps you resist lies like that?

11. How are you moved to pray in response to what you've learned about hell, angels, and demons? For instance, you might:

- Thank God for the ways He protects you.
- Pray for a nonbeliever to come to faith and avoid the torment of hell.
- Ask God to help you understand why hell exists.
- Pray for something you've been seeking for a long time, knowing that we have to pray persistently because sometimes things are happening in the spiritual realm.
- Ask your group to pray for you to resist one of Satan's lies.

Living the Life

6

To prepare for this discussion,
please read chapters 12 through 15 of *Essentials*.

SO FAR IN this study we've been concentrating on things that Christians believe are true and real. The Father and Jesus Christ are who They are; the Holy Spirit is real; angels and demons are real; heaven and hell are real. And if they're real, there's nothing more important in this life than growing to know and love and obey God more deeply each day. Therefore, the next question is, how do we do that?

It doesn't happen automatically. We walk with God by grace, not by magic.

> If you want to walk with God, if it's truly your heart's desire, you'll go for it. If, on the other hand, you're apathetic about it, you won't be inclined to go for it — all the good teaching, literature, and careful follow-up in the world won't change that. But if you have a real desire to know and serve God, by His grace you'll do just that.
>
> "But Greg," someone might protest, "it sounds like you're implying that our Christian walk is a result of human effort."
>
> Not at all.

Nevertheless, I am saying there are things only God can do, and there are things only I can do. For instance, Philippians 2:12 says, "Work out your own salvation with fear and trembling." Please note that it doesn't say to work *for* your own salvation, because that's already a gift that's been given to us by the Lord. No, it says, "Work *out* your own salvation." (*Essentials* 209–210)

In this session we're going to look at three habits we need to develop in order to grow more mature in our faith:

- Reading and loving the Bible
- Praying
- Talking about the gospel with people who don't know Jesus

1. Take this quiz on your own. (Be honest, as you won't have to share your answers with your group. There's no condemnation here, just a measure of where you are right now.)

a. During the past month, how many times have you opened a Bible and read it?

☐ Never
☐ 1–5 times
☐ 6–10 times
☐ 11–20 times
☐ More than 20 times

b. During the past week, how much time have you spent praying? (For this purpose, don't count church services, even though worshipping with a community is important.)

☐ Less than 15 minutes
☐ 15–30 minutes
☐ 30–60 minutes

☐ 1–2 hours
☐ 2–4 hours
☐ More than 4 hours

c. Let's revisit (b) with a slight change. During the past week, how much time have you spent *just* praying, not doing something else at the same time (driving, showering, and so on)? Again, don't count church services. (Of course it's important to pray all day long while we're doing other things, but this is a chance for you to notice times when you stop the treadmill and just pray.)

☐ Less than 15 minutes
☐ 15–30 minutes
☐ 30–60 minutes
☐ 1–2 hours
☐ 2–4 hours
☐ More than 4 hours

d. During the past month, how many times have you talked about Jesus Christ and/or Christian faith with a nonbeliever?

☐ 0
☐ 1
☐ 2–5
☐ More than 5

You probably know it's important to listen to what God has to say to you through the Bible, to tell God what's really in your heart through prayer, and to spread the good news about God with people who need to know it. But many of us who know that these things are important don't do them consistently. Let's explore why these habits are essential and what gets in the way of doing them consistently.

2. Read Psalm 19:7-11. Describe when you've experienced the Bible as . . .

Perfect (complete, sufficient) for your needs

Converting the soul (reviving you, transforming you in an area of weakness or sin)

Helping you grow in wisdom

Giving you a right path to follow

Causing your heart to rejoice

I can tell you from personal experience that I have put the Word of God to the test. Through the months of grieving for my son, Christopher, I have trusted in what the Bible has said. It has sustained me through the darkest hours and given me direction, hope, and comfort when I needed it most.

Little platitudes or clever sayings just won't cut it when you're in trouble or suffering, but the Word of God speaks to any and every situation. I urge you to get a good foundation in this Book, because it's only a matter of time until hardship, affliction, or even tragedy will strike you. That's not being negative; it happens in every life, without exception. But if we have a foundation in the Word of God, we'll be ready for it when it comes. Don't wait until you're in the midst of a crisis and try to catch up on all the spiritual help and insights you never had time for. Start now. Get that foundation now and take the teachings of Scripture to heart. (*Essentials* 217)

3. Following are some of the top reasons people give for not reading the Bible. How would you respond to someone who gave each of these reasons? What could help a person past each obstacle?

"I'm not much of reader. I never read much growing up."

"It was written two to three thousand years ago. A lot of it seems really foreign to me."

"I went through a period when I read the Bible a lot, but now it seems like it's all stuff I've read before, kind of stale."

"I'm very busy. When I have free time, I'm tired and just want to do something that relaxes me."

"Obtaining things," of course, isn't the only reason — or even the primary reason — we pray. (Although that might come as a surprise to some.)

Having said that, prayer most certainly is God's way of giving things to you that you need in your life. The New Testament tells us bluntly, "You do not have, because you do not ask God" (James 4:2, NIV).

Think about that. There are things God may want to give to you, do for you, and say to you, but He hasn't given you those things because you haven't asked Him.

Why is it that I never know the will of God for my life?

Could it be because you haven't asked?

Why is it that I'm never able to lead other people to Christ?

Could it be because you haven't asked?

Why am I always just barely scraping by with my finances?

Could it be because you haven't asked?

Why do I keep getting sick? Why can't I shake this infection?

Could it be because you haven't asked?

Now, I'm not suggesting here that God will always give you everything that you ask for or that He will heal every person who asks for His touch.

But He will heal some. Maybe it will be you. Have you asked Him to?

What have you got to lose? Yes, the Lord may very well say no, or perhaps wait. But He might also say yes. So go ahead and pour out your heart to Him in prayer and tell Him all your hopes and desires. (*Essentials* 231)

4. Read Matthew 6:8-13. This is the model Jesus gave His followers when they asked Him to teach them how to pray. The model begins with a reminder that we're praying to "Our Father," whose name (character) is "hallowed" or holy. When you're getting ready to start your day or when you've had a long day, how motivated are you to talk to your Father, whose

character is holy? What draws you toward Him or pushes you away?

5. Verse 10 tells us to pray for God's will to be done. The main purpose of prayer is to line up our will with God's. Do you like praying for that? Explain.

6. Verse 12 asks us to face up to our own sins and forgive others for theirs. Why are these important things to do consistently? What happens to us if we don't?

7. Verse 13 urges us to ask God to help us be wise about temptations so that we don't get too close to things that can take us down. Why do we need to pray for that?

Many of us find reasons to avoid consistently reading the Bible and praying, but we're even more determined to avoid sharing the gospel with nonbelievers. We're terrified of feeling rejected, ridiculed, a failure.

I want to communicate . . . the sheer joy of engaging another with the message of salvation in Jesus. There's no thrill that can match it.

The hardest part about evangelism is just getting started. But once you launch out and the Lord begins speaking through you, it can be one of the most exhilarating and satisfying experiences in life. You will say to yourself, *I was born for this*. Just to think that God Almighty would speak through someone like you or me is an unspeakable privilege.

The fact is, it's an honor to tell others about Jesus. Right from the start, it's a message that was designed to be shared — not hoarded. You and I were blessed to be a blessing.

In Proverbs 11:25 (NLT), Solomon wrote, "Those who refresh others will themselves be refreshed." It is refreshing to help other people learn and understand the gospel message. When we keep taking in and absorbing good teaching and strong, biblical messages but never give anything out, our knowledge can become stale and lose its vitality.

So the choice before us is really this: We can evangelize or we can fossilize. (*Essentials* 197–198)

8. a. Think of a nonbeliever in your workplace, school, family circle, gym, parents of your children's teammates in sports — anyone in your sphere of influence. What is something you've learned or discussed in this *Essentials* study that you could bring up in conversation with that person? Think of whom you could say, "I was talking with some people the other day about . . ." or "I learned something really helpful about heaven the other day . . ." or "I was talking with some people about heaven recently. What do you believe about heaven?"

    b. If you did that, what's the worst that could happen?

c. What's the best that could happen?

We will either go forward as a Christian or we will go backwards. We will either progress or regress. We will either gain ground or lose ground.

And by the way, if you stand still, you *will* lose ground.

If we want to make headway in our life in Christ, we need to make a daily commitment to grow spiritually. To progress. To learn. Not just to "hold our own" or "dig in." We need to gain ground every day. (*Essentials* 226)

9. Go before your Father in heaven, whose name is holy, and talk with Him honestly about your struggles with Bible study, prayer, and sharing the gospel.

If you're meeting with a group, have someone begin by thanking God for being your Father, praising Him for His holiness, and asking Him to help you treat Him as holy in everything you do. Tell Him you truly want to align your will with His will. Then give everyone a chance to tell God silently or aloud about the challenges they face and to ask for His help. Pray for each other to be filled with the Holy Spirit to understand the Bible, pray, and have the courage and words to talk about Jesus with nonbelievers.

Rapture, Antichrist, and Tribulation

To prepare for this discussion,
please read chapters 16 through 18 of *Essentials*.

Notes and Observations

IN 70 BC, the Roman general Titus crushed a four-year Jewish rebellion in the region the Romans called Judea. To set an example that no one in the empire could mistake, he ordered his troops to demolish Jerusalem. The Jewish temple was torched with a fire hot enough to melt the gold plating on the walls. The gold ran down into the crevices between the blocks of stone, so the soldiers tore the building apart stone by stone to retrieve the precious metal. The Jews were scattered across the empire and beyond.

Few of the ethnic groups that were Roman subjects at that time survive today as distinct ethnicities. What became of the Galli, the Iceni, or the sophisticated folk who populated North Africa before the Vandals and then the Arabs? But the Jews have endured, and on May 14, 1948, the unimaginable happened: British forces left Palestine, and David Ben-Gurion declared the new State of Israel in accordance with the 1947 UN Partition Plan.

The Old Testament prophets had predicted that one day the Jews would be able to return to their homeland, and in our day it has happened. With God, the inconceivable is not only possible but guaranteed. In this session and the next, we'll look at some of the promises God has made about the last days, the culmination of human history.

1. What goes through your mind when you think about the "last things" or "end times"? For instance, do you find the subject exciting, scary, confusing, important, boring, interesting, motivating . . . ?

When Jesus described world events prior to His return, He painted a picture of a planet stirred by strife, war, suffering, and famine in the midst of plenty, rocked by great earthquakes and ravaged by pestilence (see Luke 21:11,25-26). These events have begun, and the restoration of Israel suggests that the last days may be upon us. The next event the Bible predicts is called the Rapture of the church. The term *rapture* comes from the Latin word *rapturus*, which means "taken by force."

2. Read 1 Thessalonians 4:13-17. What does this passage tell us about who will be taken, how, when, and where?

Who:

How:

When:

Where:

3. How does Jesus describe this event in Luke 17:34-36?

In 1 Thessalonians 4:15, Paul compares the death of believers to sleep. He doesn't mean they go into some kind of "soul sleep." Rather, he's using a word picture to describe a person who has gone through death into eternal life and who is at peace. People in heaven are alive and active, worshipping and serving the Lord, waiting to be reunited with us.

4. In 1 Thessalonians 4:13-18, how does Paul want the promise of what's ahead for us to affect the way we think about death and about those who have died in faith?

5. Believers who have died before the Rapture and believers who haven't yet died will all receive renewed bodies at that time. How does Paul describe our resurrection bodies in these passages?

1 Corinthians 15:51-54

Philippians 3:20-21

Another thing that will happen is that each believer will appear before Christ's judgment seat (see 2 Corinthians 5:10). This isn't the same as the judgment unbelievers will face (more about that in session 8). It won't be a time to drag up our sins, as those will have been forgiven. Rather, it will be a time when the Lord will say to us, "What did you do with your life? What did you do with your resources? What did you do with your time and opportunities?"

At that time, crowns will be given out as rewards for faithful service — not for fame, not for glittering success, but for faithfulness in doing what God has set before us with all of our might.

6. Read 1 Corinthians 3:11-15 and 2 Corinthians 5:10. Give some examples of faithful deeds that you expect God will praise and reward.

Either right before or right after the rapture I believe a large force from the north, known as "Magog" in Scripture, will attack the nation of Israel. Shortly thereafter, a man will emerge on the scene whom the Bible describes as "the beast" and "the Antichrist."

Don't let that word *beast* fool you. He will be smooth, charismatic, skillful, and a marvelous communicator. He will come with economic solutions that will amaze everyone and with a peace treaty that the Arab nations and the Jews will both actually sign. And he will come with promises of great peace. In fact, he will be heralded by some as the messiah.

His very title, however, *Antichrist*, gives you an indication as to who he truly is. The prefix *anti*, of course, means "against," or "instead of." Many will hail him as the world's savior because of what he will be able to accomplish in such a short time.

So the Antichrist will come as a man of peace. He will do away with the monetary system as we know it today, and no one will be able to buy or sell without his mark. At the halfway point of the seven-year period known as the Tribulation, he will show his true colors, and something called "the abomination of desolation" will take place. This will occur after the third Jewish temple has been rebuilt in Israel, and the Antichrist will erect an image of himself and command worship. (*Essentials* 260–261)

7. a. Read 2 Thessalonians 2:1-12, which describes the "man of lawlessness" (NIV) — the Antichrist. What does this passage tell us about him?

b. Why do you think masses of people are drawn to leaders like this? What do you think they're looking for?

8. In 1 Thessalonians 5:6-8, Paul describes how we should respond to the knowledge that these things could occur within our lifetime. What does he tell us to do and not do?

To be sober means that you are to be clearheaded. You are to be alert, sane, and steady, with your eyes open. Don't be drunk or careless, and don't let yourself be preoccupied or overcome with cares and worries. Be awake and alert. (*Essentials* 270–271)

9. Give some practical examples of what being awake and sober means in your life.

The Tribulation will be a time when:

- God will send violent judgments upon the earth.
- Many Jews and non-Jews will come to faith in Christ.
- These believers will be intensely persecuted for their faith.
- Two witnesses (Moses and Elijah, or men like them) will have powerful ministries to draw people to faith. They will be killed and their bodies publicly left to decay.

Of course, even today in various parts of the world, Christians are being persecuted. Some are dying for their faith. During the Cultural Revolution in China, the persecution, torture, and killing were so bad that some Christians thought the Tribulation had begun, and they were shocked that they hadn't been taken in the Rapture. So we shouldn't be complacent and expect to be immune from suffering and death.

10. What do you think it says about God that He will remove the church from the earth before the Tribulation?

The Bible's prophecies of the end times refer to several specific nations, including Israel, Iran (formerly called Persia), Libya, probably Sudan, probably Russia, probably China, and possibly Europe. America isn't mentioned. This could be because the United States will decline as a world power before then; the United States will be shattered in some disaster, such as a nuclear attack; or so many Americans will turn to Christ before the Rapture that the nation will collapse economically and militarily when they are taken. We don't know. But what American Christians should do is pray, reach out to the lost, and turn to God with great passion so that revival rather than disaster is what removes our nation from the world stage.

11. In light of what you've been studying, what do you think you should pray for? Make a list.

At the end of the Tribulation, a battle called Armageddon will be fought in the valley of Megiddo in Israel. During that battle, Jesus Christ will return to the earth. This return is called the Second Coming. In our final session, we'll look into the Second Coming and what will follow it.

12. Talk with God about the emotions this discussion has raised in you. Pray also for the things and people you listed under question 11. Ask Him to show you how to live a more alert and sober life, eagerly looking forward to what He has in store for you.

Jesus Returns to Reign

8

**To prepare for this discussion,
please read chapters 19 and 20 of *Essentials*.**

THE VALLEY OF Megiddo in Israel is a vast plain where many battles were fought in Old Testament times. King Saul died there. In 1799, Napoleon called it "the most natural battleground on the whole earth" because of its size and flatness. And one day it will be the setting for the greatest battle of all time: Armageddon. In this session, we'll look at the glorious future in store for us after that battle is won.

1. How do you picture Armageddon? (Revelation 16:16-21 tells us some of what we know about it.)

2. During that battle, Jesus Christ will return to the earth. This return is called the Second Coming. What can we learn about the Second Coming from Revelation 19:11-14? How is Jesus described?

3. How will Jesus' second coming be different from the way He came the first time, two thousand years ago?

Jesus' second coming will be seen by everyone. He will wear many crowns because He is Lord over all the universe, and His robe will be spattered with blood to remind us of the death He suffered when He came the first time.

4. Jesus will come with the armies of heaven (see Revelation 19:14). These will include all of His people who have died and all those who will have joined him at the Rapture. How do you picture that moment? What goes through your mind?

5. Read Luke 12:35-40. Jesus speaks here of servants whose master has gone to a wedding, which in the first century could last for days. Jesus tells these servants to have their long garments girded up at their waists, as a man would do to prepare to work or fight, while they wait for their master to return.

a. What does it mean for us today to have our garments girded up and our lamps burning (see verse 35)? What is Jesus saying about the mindset and habits we should have as we wait for Him to come?

b. In verse 37, He says we should be "watching." In practical terms, what does watching for Him involve? Should we be staring up at the sky or at the computer screen?

Jesus will return with us and defeat Satan, the Antichrist, and their followers (humans and demons). Then Jesus—with us—will reign on earth for a thousand years (see Revelation 20:1-6). *Mille annis* is Latin for "a thousand years," and so we call this period the Millennium.

6. What picture of life during the Millennium do you get from these passages?

Isaiah 2:3-4

Isaiah 11:6-9

Psalm 72:7-8

There will still be people alive on earth who didn't embrace Christ, but believers will reign over them and their descendants, so they won't be able to corrupt the world. We will have our resurrection bodies, but they will still have ordinary ones. Satan will be imprisoned, but at the end of the thousand years, he will be released for one last chance to deceive people. Amazingly, there will still be people around who will prefer Satan's kingship to Jesus'. They will rebel, but they will be defeated and face the Great White Throne judgment.

7. Read Revelation 20:12-15. How does it describe the Great White Throne judgment? How will this be different from the judgment believers will have already faced? (See question 6 in session 7.)

The grand finale will be when heaven comes to earth and the two become one.

> God won't abandon His creation, He will *restore* it. His perfect plan, according to Ephesians 1:10, is to bring all things in heaven *and on earth* together under one head, the Lord Jesus Christ.
>
> In his excellent book, *Heaven*, Randy Alcorn writes, "We won't go to Heaven and leave Earth behind. Rather, God will bring Heaven and Earth together into the same dimension, with no wall of separation, no armed angels to guard Heaven's perfection from sinful mankind."[4] (*Essentials* 323–324)

8. Read Revelation 21:1-5. What do you see here that you look forward to?

9. a. God plans to restore the earth rather than scrap it. What does this say about His attitude toward the earth He's created?

b. If He thinks the earth is worth restoring, what are the implications for us today? Should we take special care of it, or does that not matter because He's going to renovate it anyway?

So to recap, the last things include:

- The Rapture of the church
- Believers receiving rewards at the judgment seat of Christ
- The rise of the Antichrist
- The seven-year Great Tribulation
- The battle of Armageddon
- The second coming of Christ
- The Millennium
- The rebellion of unbelievers and the Great White Throne judgment
- The new heavens and earth

Everybody needs something to live for. Everyone needs a driving passion, something that gets him or her out of bed in the morning. . . .

We have all been given one life to use for the glory of God during our lifespan on earth, be it long or short. While most of us know the date of our birth, very few of us know the date of our death. And in between birth and death we have that little dash in the middle.

That line, that dash, is our lifetime, our one opportunity to invest for the glory of our Creator and our God. (*Essentials* 333, 337)

10. Does your hope of Jesus' return and the new heavens and earth affect what you're living for? If so, how? If not, what are you living for?

11. How are you moved to pray in response to what you've learned about the last things? If you like, you can go through Revelation 21 and praise God for each thing He says about Himself and each thing He says He's going to do. If you're meeting with a group, each person can take a verse in turn. For example, "Lord, You are the Alpha and the Omega, the A to Z. Everything begins and ends with You. Thank You for Your promise to let me drink from the spring of the water of life."

Leader's Notes

IF THIS IS your first time leading a small-group discussion, don't worry. You don't need to know the perfect answers to the questions, and you don't need to be a Bible expert. What you do need is a willingness to read the corresponding portions of *Essentials* each week, look up the Bible passages you'll be studying, think about the questions ahead of time, and read these leader's notes. You also need to ask the Holy Spirit to work in your life and the lives of your group members.

Leader's Job Description

Your role is to:

- *Help people bond as a group*, especially if they don't know each other well. The first question in each session usually invites people to say a little about themselves as they start thinking about the topic at hand. (In one case, there's a quiz for them to do on their own.) If people are shy at first, you can go first in answering question 1. Give a genuine answer, and keep it under one minute long.

Ask everyone else to keep their answers to a minute rather than tell long stories so that this question doesn't consume all of your time. The intent here is break the ice and get to know things about each other that don't usually come out in small talk. (Normally, you should *not* go first in answering the questions. Question 1 is the exception. If you routinely answer the questions, people will stay silent and act like your audience.)

- *Keep the discussion moving.* Encourage people to have a conversation rather than just going around the circle and sharing answers to each question. You can ask follow-up questions such as, "Why do you think that's the case?" "Can you say more about that?" "What do others think?" "Is there a particular place in Acts that supports that idea?" and "Does the book shed any light on this?"

- *Keep the group on track* when it's tempted to go off on a tangent. If people get bogged down on a question or go off topic, you can say, "I'm going to interrupt here and bring us back to the text." "Does anyone else have thoughts on question 2?" or "Let's go on to the next question. Could someone read it aloud?"

- *Make sure everyone gets a chance to talk* and that no one dominates. It's not necessary that every person respond aloud to every question, but every person should have the chance to do so. Sometimes it's necessary to interrupt a talkative person and say, "Thanks, Joe. What do others think?" You, too, should not dominate the discussion.

- *Make sure the discussion remains respectful.* See the ground rules under the upcoming "Guiding the Discussion" section.

- *Pray for your group.* Ask for the Holy Spirit to fill each person, increase their faith and courage, and empower them to share the gospel with those around them. Many of them may never have led someone to Christ. Ask God to do more through them than they can imagine.

Preparing for the Discussion

Read the chapters from *Essentials* before each group meeting. If you can, work through your own responses to the discussion questions ahead of time. Even though you won't be sharing your answers each time, thinking through the questions will help you think of follow-up questions.

Guiding the Discussion

A few ground rules can make people comfortable discussing what they really think:

- *Confidentiality:* Whatever is said in the group stays in the group. Nothing is to be repeated to those who weren't there.
- *Honesty:* We're not here to impress each other. We're here to grow and to know each other.
- *Respect:* Disagreement is welcome; disrespect is not.

Ask for a volunteer to read each question aloud before you discuss it. In some cases, it will be helpful to have someone read aloud the text between the questions.

Encourage people to talk to each other rather than coming to only you. When someone shares an answer, avoid replying with your own views. Instead, ask what others think. If someone says something seriously unbiblical, give others in the group a chance to say what is true rather than doing it yourself. If no one does, say something such as, "There's a Bible passage that sheds light on what we're discussing," and then tell them the Scripture to look for and ask a group member to read it aloud. Do your best to let the group arrive at what the Bible teaches, and take the role of teacher yourself only as a last resort.

Likewise, avoid the temptation to answer a question if others are silent. Don't be afraid of silence. Wait for the group. People often need time to think. If you answer the questions, people will learn to wait for you, and discussion will be squelched. Sometimes it's helpful to rephrase the question in your own words. Then wait for others' responses.

There isn't enough space in this guide to give you suggested answers for all of the discussion questions, and in many cases group members will be talking about their own lives, so there isn't a single right answer. Therefore, in the following notes, we've chosen some questions from each session to address. In some cases, these notes will give guidance on how to handle a question, and in other cases, they will suggest answers to questions that might be especially difficult. These answers aren't meant to be exhaustive, nor are they (in most cases) the only right answer. They're meant to help you if the group gets stuck or off track.

Session 1

Question 4. If you have a group of Christians who are eager to share their stories, you may need to ask people to keep the stories brief so that everyone gets a chance to share. If you have some new believers or nonbelievers, let a few of the others share their stories, but then give airtime to those who haven't knowingly experienced God's help. Allow some safe space for them to share their questions and needs.

Question 5. "Is it not from the mouth of the Most High that woe and well-being proceed?" (Lamentations 3:38) is a powerful statement of God's sovereignty even in times of tragedy. How can a good God allow woe? The writer of Lamentations believes that God is good and allows woe: "Through the LORD's mercies we are not consumed, because His compassions fail not. . . . Great is Your faithfulness. . . . The LORD is good to those who wait for Him" (verses 22-23,25). God doesn't cause evil, but He creates free beings (human and angelic) who choose evil, and He allows their evil and even brings good out of it. This is a deep paradox and doesn't minimize the suffering of those who don't know why God has allowed something in their lives. Allow those questions and hurts to surface and be voiced. Don't let group members give pat answers or advice to each other.

Question 7. A wholesome dread of God should motivate us to do what He says and not indulge our impulses. It should make us more afraid of sin than of failure or what people think. If we fear God, we need not fear anything else.

Session 2

Question 2. The Word (Jesus) was God. All things were made through Him and by Him. Only He has the authority to forgive sins, as sin is by definition against God. All things "consist," or hold together, in Him.

Question 3. Jesus reconciled all things to Himself, to God. He makes believers holy, blameless, and above reproach. He made peace between God and believers first of all, and He also makes peace among believers. In Ephesians 2:11-22, Paul talks about the peace Jesus makes between Jewish and Gentile believers.

Question 6. Jesus wants us to go boldly to the throne of grace (God's throne) and ask for mercy (instead of the punishment we deserve) and grace (the welcome and good gifts we don't deserve, including the power to become like Christ).

Question 7. Jesus has always been the Son of God. He and the Father are one in "substance" — they are both God. We don't become equal to Jesus when we are adopted as God's children. We do become "partakers of the divine nature" (2 Peter 1:4), but that's not the same as being gods equal to God the Son.

Question 9. For example, the path of doing what I want as long as I don't hurt anybody else. (This makes me a god, even if I'm a pretty nice god, and I'm kidding myself if I think I won't end up hurting others.) Or the path of being a likeable, respectable person so that other people will think well of me. (This puts others' opinions ahead of God's agenda.)

Question 10. The question of how a good God can allow woe (session 1) is answered best by looking at the woe God was willing to experience voluntarily, purely out of love for us. Whatever tragedy we have suffered, He has suffered equally. He's not just up there in a comfortable heaven sending suffering on helpless humans.

Question 11. Jesus did feel overwhelmed with sorrow while He waited in the garden to be arrested (see Mark 14:34). He felt frustrated at unbelief (see 9:19). And Isaiah tells us how much Jesus was acquainted with grief. But His hurt was never egotistical self-pity that wanted others to pay, His frustration wasn't hostile, and His overwhelming sorrow didn't lead Him to despair or stop loving. *Jesus Christ Superstar* diminishes Him to our size. That's easy to do.

Session 3

Question 1. Part of the Force's appeal is that humans can use it by exerting their own wills. It puts us in control. But the Holy Spirit is a Person with His own will, and we can't control or use Him. Whenever we slide into thinking the Spirit's job is to empower us to get our way, we're ceasing to think like Christians.

Question 2. The Son is a man in the water. The Spirit descends on Him like a dove. The Father speaks from heaven. The Holy Spirit isn't the man in the water, and He isn't the one who is speaking from heaven about His Son. It's hard to picture them all as one Being when they are in action separately like this, but God is beyond our mental pictures.

Question 3. We can't summon the Spirit and make Him do what we want by our wills. He doesn't come and go at our word. We can ask Him respectfully to do things we think are in line with His will. We can offer to cooperate with Him in what He wants to do. We can make space in our lives to listen for His marching orders. But we need to treat Him with respect, with even more respect than we would give the human person we most admire.

Question 5. The Spirit likes to work through people. He doesn't need us to cooperate with Him, but God has chosen to make the world in such a way that the Spirit often waits for humans to cooperate with Him. We do this by praying for Him to convince people, having relationship with others up close so that they can see what a Christian's life is like, and planting seeds of thought about the gospel that the Spirit can use to convince people. God holds us responsible for doing our part.

Question 6. The Force doesn't improve people's character and make them better human beings. It gives them power to pursue their goals, good or bad. One doesn't "use the Force" to become more loving. By contrast, love is at the top of the Spirit's agenda. And there is no "dark side" of the Holy Spirit; the "dark side" comes from other spirits.

Some people are more interested in the gifts of the Spirit than in the fruit of the Spirit. Paul has stern things to say to such people in 1 Corinthians.

Question 7. Busyness and distraction are most people's biggest barriers to abiding in Christ. There are lots of practical things we can do to push against distraction. For instance, we can choose silence in the car or at home, turning off the radio, the music player, the things with screens. For one month, try turning these off during your commute or while you're getting ready to leave in the morning. Go screen-free for twenty-four hours every two weeks. Your head will really talk back to you about this! But that's the point.

Session 4

Question 3. The precious stones echo God's promise in Isaiah 54:11-12. They also reflect the idea that the Holy City is the bride of Christ adorned for her wedding (see Revelation 21:2). In the first century, it was customary for Jewish brides to adorn themselves with gold and jewels, and this bride puts Babylon's finery (see 17:4) to shame. Babylon, the city of the world, is obsessed with getting rich through exploitative business (see 18:11-17), but all of that will be swept away and replaced with a city that is even more beautiful and bountiful with true riches. God's people will lack nothing good and beautiful, and we won't have to strive and compete with each other to have it.

Question 5. Encourage people to let their imaginations go and to dig down beneath even distorted desires to the true longing underneath. For instance, the person who craves clothes and shoes and accessories may have a deep longing to be radiantly beautiful and to create beauty through color and design in endless new ways. The person troubled by sexual temptation may yearn for excitement or beauty or a deep intimacy that isn't marred by the kinds of disappointments that intimacy with a real person in this life inevitably brings. A person may long for the vibrant energy of eternal youth, time and training to express creativity, the satisfaction of good work well done, the power to make a lasting difference in the world, or true love that never fails.

Question 6. One of the very early distortions of the gospel, just a generation after the Bible was written, was the idea that the soul is pure but the body is corrupt. But Paul and Jesus were very clear that evil comes out of the heart (see Matthew 15:18-20), not from the body. It's good to have bodies — we were made to have bodies — so we need to learn to be thankful to God for them. What we do with our bodies has great spiritual significance. That's why sexual immorality and gluttony are sins; things we do with our bodies affect our souls. Women in particular struggle with loving their bodies if they don't meet the world's standards of perfection. But Paul asks us to look forward to resurrected bodies and value our bodies now, even though they're not perfect.

Question 8. People may be shy about sharing their dreams. If they are, you as leader can prime the pump by sharing something you've always wanted to do. Write? Paint? Build things? Finish a project you got stuck on years ago? Finish the education or do the work you abandoned when you needed to focus on paying bills or raising a family?

Question 9. Great food is a bodily pleasure, but even beyond that, feasting implies celebration with other people. Heaven will involve not just worship of and intimacy with God but also friendship with other people. And Jesus will be there at the head of the table.

Question 11. It's nearly impossible to put to death our sinful desires and replace them with nothing. It's far easier to do it by cultivating better desires. We need to replace bad habits not with nothing but with good habits. Filling our thoughts with hope of heaven and deliberately cultivating desires that will be fulfilled in heaven will crowd out sinful thoughts and desires.

Question 12. Heaven is a place where God — not self, status, achievement, spouse, children, possessions, perfection, power, or pleasure — is worshipped. Heaven is a place where we will have enough, and desiring heaven is inconsistent with obsessively desiring anything on earth. We don't have to be wrathfully or spitefully angry at people who block our earthly goals if we count those goals not as things we *have to have* but as secondary to the things we have to have — and will have — in heaven.

Question 13. For example, setting aside time to read passages in Revelation about heaven each day for a week or two can help foster a healthy hope of heaven.

Session 5

Question 2. Repetition is often an indicator of importance, and *torment* is repeated four times. That seems to be the key thing about hell. *Flame* is part of the picture of torment. *A great gulf* indicates that getting out of hell once one is in it isn't an option. The rich man seems conscious of being in torment; he hasn't ceased to exist.

Question 3. "The sin of this man was not his wealth; the sin of this man was that he had no time for God. You might say that he was possessed by his possessions" (*Essentials* 148). He didn't care about Lazarus because his mind was full of himself.

Question 4. For most people in the developed world, the Bible is readily available. The U.S. is deluged with Christian media. So here, at least, the problem isn't lack of available information; it's lack of interest in seeking and understanding the information. Still, part of our job as Christians is to use our words and actions to spark nonbelievers' interest in the available information. Also, there are parts of the world where information about the gospel isn't available, and it's our job to support ministries that provide that information.

Question 5. Lots of people feel this way. This question gives them a chance to say so. Don't argue them down, but have a dialogue about page 154 in *Essentials*, which says that people themselves choose hell if they don't want to spend eternity with God.

Question 6. Sometimes angels appear as men, but the seraphim appear to Isaiah as six-winged creatures. Angels are far more likely to be terrifying than cute. Praising God is part of their job, especially praising His holiness — His otherness and moral purity. Another part of their job is to be messengers from God. (In fact, *angel* comes from the Greek word for messenger.)

Session 6

Question 1. Give people three or four minutes on their own to complete the survey if they didn't do it at home. Don't ask them to share their answers, but do allow a few minutes to debrief the experience. You might ask, "What did you notice about yourself?" or "Which of these disciplines are hard for you to practice consistently?" or "How does a self-assessment like that make you feel? Motivated? Discouraged?"

Question 3. Take the reasons one at a time. Rather than making fun of them (because there may be some in your group who are making those excuses), try to come up with serious ways of helping people in each case. What resources would help a person who is struggling with the time and culture barrier? Who in your church could recommend resources for laypeople? Another suggestion is for group members to start with one of the Gospels rather than Genesis. One chapter per day or even one story per day in one of the Gospels — read and thought about — can establish a habit of Bible reading. The excuse of busyness, too, needs a serious response. If a person is too busy to spend ten minutes a day with God, there's a question about his or her priorities.

Question 5. This may seem like a surprising question, but its purpose is to expose the heart. Do we really want God's will to be done? Do we trust His will? Or do we really want *our* will to be done? Invite participants to think about this in relation to various aspects of their lives: work, family, health, finances, and so on. It's better to admit we're praying through gritted teeth for God's will on our finances than to have that in our heart but not face it.

Question 8. This gives you a chance to review what you've discussed in previous sessions. Ask participants, "Is there anything you learned about heaven that a nonbeliever might be interested in? What about something you learned about God in session 1 or something you've learned about Jesus? Hell is a controversial subject; for certain nonbelievers it might be interesting. Could you float the idea that people choose hell and see what a non-believing friend says? Or maybe offer the Asimov quotation about heaven and ask your nonbelieving friend how he or she pictures heaven, if at all." Help group members identify nonbelievers who might be open to such a conversation.

Session 7

Question 2. Who: Both believers who have died and believers who are still alive. How: Jesus will come from heaven and command the dead to rise, and those who are still alive will be caught up in the air with them. When: It says nothing about when! Where: The passage speaks of "in the clouds" and "in the air."

Question 5. Our bodies will be immortal, imperishable (they won't die or age or get sick), and glorious (beautiful, radiant) like Jesus' resurrected body. Like His body, they will have mass and occupy space and be capable of eating food, but their relationship to the current laws of physics may be different; the resurrected Jesus could pass through locked doors (see Luke 24:36-43).

Question 6. These will include loving actions of all kinds, especially love for difficult people, children and other vulnerable people, spouses in stressful times, nonbelievers, and people who don't repay us with love. The faithful deeds might involve sharing the gospel with others, whether we are thanked or rejected. Some might revolve around great self-sacrifice and simple gratitude and small acts of service to build up the body of Christ: cleaning floors and painting walls and listening to people who need to be heard.

Questions 8 and 9. He tells us to wake up, not to fall into drifting through our Christian lives. He tells us to be sober, self-controlled—to deal with our anxieties and our temptations to excess so that they don't control us. We need clear heads. We need to defend ourselves from spiritual attack not with hostility but with faith and hope. For some of us, soberness means ruling our emotions (anger, worry, and so on) rather than letting them rule us. For others, it means ruling our desires for pleasure and excitement rather than letting them rule us.

Session 8
Question 3.

> In his first coming, when He arrived in that manger in Bethlehem, He was wrapped in swaddling cloths. In His second coming, He will be clothed royally, in a robe spattered in blood. In His first coming He was surrounded by animals and shepherds. In His second coming He will be accompanied by saints and angels. At His first coming the door of the inn was closed to Him. But in His second coming the door of the heavens is opened to Him. The first time He came He was the Lamb of God, dying for the sin of the world. At His second coming He is the ferocious Lion of the Tribe of Judah, bringing judgment.
>
> And notice this: When He returns, Jesus will not be alone. (*Essentials* 315–316)

You may want to make sure everyone understands the difference between the Rapture and the Second Coming. The

Rapture happens before the Antichrist appears and the Tribulation begins. The Second Coming happens at the battle of Armageddon at the end of the seven-year Tribulation. At the Rapture, Jesus appears in the clouds but doesn't appear on the earth. At the Second Coming, He is bodily on earth.

Question 5. Having our clothes girded up is a word picture for being ready to work (to do whatever God gives us to do) or fight (to resist the temptations of the enemy). It means we're not practicing our faith for an hour on Sundays and then living the rest of the week with hardly a thought for the work Christ has for us in these last days. We practice His presence regularly rather than giving our whole day to busyness or entertainment. Having our lamps burning also means we're ready to go with Christ whenever He comes. "Watching" doesn't mean peering at the sky or reading end times blogs; it means being spiritually awake, not lazy or distracted. We don't live for money or status like everybody else. Loving God and others is our top priority because we could go at any time.

Question 7. The Great White Throne judgment will be for nonbelievers—those who have rejected Jesus Christ and His forgiveness and salvation. They will stand before Christ and give an accounting of their lives. They will have to face the just consequences of their wrong actions. For them, Christ will sit as the terrifying Judge of the truth of who they are at the core of their being. By contrast, those who believe in Jesus Christ and have embraced His offer of forgiveness and salvation won't have to face this judgment. They will have stood before His judgment seat earlier, not to be condemned for their wrongdoing but to be rewarded for their right doing. Their wrongdoing will have been forgiven. For them, Jesus Christ will be the person who took on Himself the terrifying consequences of sin.

Question 10. Allow some silence for people to think about their answers. It's good to search our hearts and find the truth of what we're really living for. If people have trouble with this, ask them to think about what they spend money on and what they tend to think about most of the day.

Notes

1. Rosemarie Jarski, *Words from the Wise: Over 6,000 of the Smartest Things Ever Said* (New York: Sky Horse Publishing, 2007), 18.

2. C. S. Lewis, *The Problem of Pain* (Clearwater, FL: Touchstone Books, 1996), 134.

3. J. I. Packer, http://johnsnotes.com/archives/end_times/03_05_04_Hell2.shtml.

4. Randy Alcorn, *Heaven* (Wheaton, IL: Tyndale, 2004), 88.

Other Books by Greg Laurie

Visit www.kerygmapublishing.com

KERYGMA
PUBLISHING